I0617398

something new to say

words of spirit, faith and celebration for Advent and Christmas

bronwyn angela white

Philip
Garside
Publishing Ltd.

Copyright © 2017 & 2022 Bronwyn Angela White

www.spiritandfaithwords.com

All rights reserved.

This collection was first published as an eBook in 2017 and in print in 2018.

Cover design and photograph
© Bronwyn Angela White

Author photo © Warwick Metcalfe

Paperback International 2nd edition 2022:
ISBN 9781991027375

Also available

New Zealand paperback: ISBN 9781991027368

Paperback print-on-demand USA: ISBN 9798362511333

PDF: ISBN 9781991027382

ePub: ISBN 9781991027399

Philip Garside Publishing Ltd
PO Box 17160
Wellington 6147
New Zealand

books@pgpl.co.nz — www.pgpl.co.nz

Contents

About the words

Everything in this book—including the poetry—was written to be read, presented or performed aloud.

Several pieces were written as litanies, with 'the leader' beginning each section and 'the people' responding with the lines in italics.

On the page, some of the liturgical works will seem repetitive. In *you who delight me*, I grouped items with similar themes or formats to show how simply a basic outline or idea can be varied for different situations.

In this book, I've grouped writing by type—prayers, reflections, blessings etc—and especially with the prayers you might like to pick and mix paragraphs to create a different form or format for your occasion.

When the ideas are fresh, you can use a familiar form to introduce inclusive, liberal and theologically progressive concepts to a more conservative audience.

I hope these resources will be enjoyed and shared by anyone who sees the sacred in the everyday.

Copyright and usage

You are welcome to use with acknowledgement—and if necessary, slightly adapt for the occasion—all this liturgical material.

All work in this book is licensed under a Creative Commons Attribution- NonCommercial-ShareAlike 3.0 New Zealand License.

Poems and Prayers

A world safe for a new born baby

We gather on this holy day
Whānau and friends
Family of blood and of choice
to celebrate the birth of a special child
in whom Christians believe
GodSpirit was especially present
—as GodSpirit can be in us.

Some of us have come from afar
with our gifts, our wisdom, our presence.
Some have come from the nearby fields,
a brief break from the busyness of our lives.

May we open the doors of our hearts
and lives and communities
to welcome the strangers or the angels
to welcome questions and uncertainty
to be catalysts for discovery;

May we open our hearts and our hands
to act for a just and peaceful world
a world safe for a new born baby
prepared for the rebirth of hope.

Emergency responders & peace-keepers

On this day of rebirth and celebration
we think of emergency, medical and
law enforcement personnel,
the firefighters and funeral directors on call,
working this weekend and throughout the holiday season;
dealing with fatal motor accidents, suicides,
and alcohol-induced violence.

May the joy and hope of Christmas touch hearts and minds
grown cynical from dealing with human folly and failure.

We hold in our hearts the peace-keepers and peace-makers,
those who bring aid to the ravaged and war-torn;
the agencies and individuals who bring food and medication,
who assist communities in self-development,
in clean water and vital crop projects,
who help make the desert bloom.

We think of Christians around the world,
gathering to acknowledge the birth of a baby,
a child of peace, in a world that still knows little peace,
as many, who claim to follow the way of Jesus,
instead pursue a path of exclusion and wall-building.

May the love and joy of Christmas
touch hearts and minds of all who seek the Light,
whatever their faith or creed.

Entertaining angels

From Hebrews 13:2—
"Be not forgetful to entertain strangers:
for thereby some have entertained angels unawares."

(i)
Breathe in
Breathe out

Still, now
Let the angels brush you
cool clear spirits dancing
across your skin

Breathe in
gilding the air as they still you
—lips, tongue, throat, lungs
limbs, organs, blood-heat, pulse-beat—
angels in your mind
tapping your fingers
dancing in your toes

Breathe out
release them
let them be borne off on airy wings.

Breathe in—out.
You are ready, now, to entertain them
strange as they seem
syntax of fire and air.

(ii)
They sail towards me on the harbour
white angels
skimming dawn-gilt waves

As I make coffee
they float—just through the window

and on the weekend
as I munch my toast
they race towards the Strait
white wings unfurled
skimming the dance-floor of the up-side-down sky.

Bright red and buzzing
like an anxious mother
the rescue angel
rotor-blades the sky
slicing the clouds
searching...

Breathe in. Breathe out.
Do not forget them.

(iii)
Do not forget the strangers
at your door
as you raise your glass
toast the new year
the past
the absent friends
the auld acquaintances
—the birth of a long-ago child.

Do not forget the strangers
in the crowd
the watchful ones
the furtive, awkward,
battered,
manic ones
in the advent of summer holidays, of holy days.

Do not forget
—as you laugh and embrace and wish all well
and spill goodwill like crumpled wrapping paper
laugh at unfunny cracker jokes
and pull each other's legs
as you thank the host
and season the feast with good cheer

that there are angels
waiting
answering phones, maybe
waiting to drive you home
offering refuge.

(iv)
Sometimes they come quietly
these entertaining angels
falling into your path
like stars
as the sun darkens

or—
Suddenly
with a blast of trumpets,
drumbeats, cymbals, castanets,
plucking the strings
of your heart,
harp, harpsichord, mandolin, cello
strumming and humming and
harping on
when you least expect them

nagging and clapping and
clicking their fingers to
snap you awake!
Tooting and hooting at your complacency
laughing your good intentions into action
looting your heart
for the strangeness lurking there

teasing and taunting
turning the stranger to friend
ruffling your feathers, tossing you to the winds
scooping you up, stroking you
with their wings.

(v)

Do not forget the heavenly host
coming in clouds of glory
brightening the air
spilling like stars, like champagne
skimming the sea
like yachts, like kites

skirting the crowds
searching the season
for strangers and welcomers

strumming and twanging and singing
frightening sheep, stunning the shepherds
spangling the sky
exhorting the earth to embrace
peace and goodwill
syntax of word and flesh

Spreading their wings
forming a Cross
pointing to west and east
as they light the path
to Bethlehem
—to Jerusalem, to Galilee
midwifing at the birth
foreshadowing resurrection.

Be not forgetful of angels.

Strange as they seem
entertain them:
let the cool spirits dance you.

Do not let them take you
unaware.

In this season of Advent and wonder

In this season of Advent and wonder
we celebrate our covenant to be inclusive.
We give thanks for the communities we've created
despite our varied backgrounds, cultures and beliefs.
We proudly fly our rainbow banners
and decorate our Christmas trees,
giving thanks that we are family:
extended, reconstituted, recreated
that there is room for us here
in our diversity and similarity.

We give thanks for life
brief as the grass, and for life everlasting.

We think of those who're anxious about people they love:
those who're separated by distance, physical or emotional.
We hold in our hearts all who mourn the loss of loved ones
through broken relationships
through the grief of personalities distorted by ill-health—
and especially those bereaved by death.

As we await, once more, the birthing-day
of the one who brings good news
        who cares for careless and uncared for;
as we await the gift of family, lovers, friends
the sacrament of food and wine set at our tables
        or shared around the barbecue
let us think forward to Easter and the Resurrection.

May our lives be candles of peace;
        may we light up our world and prepare the way.

Let us be the gift we long for

Sometimes our lives seem like an endless Advent:
Always waiting,
    being ready,
    hustling, preparing
for the big moment, the fulfilment, the dream come true.

When will there be peace on earth,
when will poverty be history
our inbox full of good news, happy hashtags,
    joy instead of hate speech?
How long before we need no ribbons, white or red or green?

And we wait.
How long, we ask, how long?

This Advent, may we *be* the promised kept,
the word made flesh, the kingdom come
not just on high and holy days
but in ordinary times as well.

So may we enjoy this time of preparation
    thrilling to angel song and sparkling lights
    Snoopy's Christmas and *Silent Night*;
    may the little boy drum for us, pum-a-pum-pum
    and the wise ones' gifts be ours
birthing each day
the Christ of our imagination.

Let us be the gift we long for
long after the paper's discarded and the cards are put away;
be the love that keeps on loving:
joy in our world, day after day.

Love born in us this day

We give thanks for this season of celebration and remembering
when, each year
we pause to make a small space for wonder in our lives
to let in a baby-sized gleam of hope
to watch the stars bursting in the sky
and share the communion
of wine and bread and being together
the gifts of receiving and giving.

We hold the mystery in our hearts
and give thanks for renewal and togetherness,
for all that is fresh and good and loving in our lives.

We hold in our hearts those for whom this is a time of sadness
Our hearts go out to all who have lost loved ones
in holiday seasons past;
the lonely, the homeless, the bereaved.
Despite the pain, may hope be born in them again.

We give thanks for the angels who sing to us
the families who nurture us
the stars that guide us
wise ones, shepherds and kaumātua
who show us the way

We give thanks that we can put down our cares
our gifts and responsibilities, our tributes and concerns,
and for this moment
we're engulfed in love:
Love born in us this day.

Red tape, red ribbon

In our prayers of solidarity,
we pray for our Members of Parliament,
and each week we name and pray for two of them
and the people in their electorates.

Today we pray for all MPs struggling with their consciences
over what is just and what is politic;

for the officials who advise them;
and the many who turn policy into practice

striving to enact the theories, the intentions,
the well-meant regulations
in ways that liberate and heal
rather than frustrate and bind.

We hold in our hearts the public servants,
desk-bound and frontline.

This Advent season
may the red tape of bureaucracy
be transformed into the Christmas ribbon of generosity,

that the initiatives and campaigns
and packages
may become gifts
of spirit and liberation,
justice and transformation.

Refugee child

As we celebrate the birth of a refugee child,
born in odd circumstances, of dubious parentage,
let us pray for this earth and its peoples.

We think of refugees, seeking freedom and a new life
fearful of the welcome they'll receive
in the countries who take them in.

We hold in our hearts
all those who are away from home, but not from choice, tonight:
     women and children who've fled to Refuge,
     men in prison, far from whānau and friends,
     hoping for loved ones to visit—or dreading it,
people who can't get into their homes
following earthquakes and natural disasters
refugees carrying their world with them,
hoping for at best, a welcome;
     at least, a dry place to sleep and an end to war
     and destruction and persecution.

We think of the peoples of Israel and Palestine
in their twin desire for a rightful home;
we feel for the people of the city of Bethlehem
so flooded with Christian tourists this season
that once again all the hotels are full.

And we pray for all the world.
We hold these people
– their hopes and fears, their comfort and safety –
in our hearts.
May ours be a society, a country,
where the walls of inclusion aren't built too high,
where "no vacancy" signs are unlit.

Signs of home

As we await, once more,
the birth day celebration of the child
who grew to be prophet, mystic, healer
who brought good news
who thoughtfully yet thoroughly broke the rules
    —social, political, religious—
    that bound the men and women of his time
who cared for the careless and the uncared for
who took time to see the sparrows fall
    observe the lilies of the field
    comfort a friend;

As we await this rebirth in our lives, these signs of home,
so often we are restless:
    as if the waiting takes too long, rushed
    as if there was too much to do
    —the shopping, the cooking,
    the hasty wrapping of these birth day gifts—
too stressed, to see and to create the signs of home
in our homes, in our workplaces, in our lives
    —these sprigs of green.

As we await the Christ-life breaking into our world
let us take time to hear the sparrow and the bellbird,
observe the Christmas decoration
    of red pōhutukawa and golden gorse and tree fern's green
to be still
in the joy of friends' company,
    in sharing celebration and remembering.

May our homes and our lives
    glisten with summer sun
    chime to tūī's carol
    and sparkle with streams of joy.

We wait in the silence of this whare kōwhanga

Prayer on Christmas Eve

We wait in the quiet of this whare kōwhanga
for the whānautanga of a new day,
a new beginning—we hope—for all people.

It is not a silent thing, this quiet:
for in it are echoes, memories, birdsong
the rustle of hay in a manger and mice in the straw.
It is a quiet reverberating with the music of the spheres
with choirs of angels,
with the vast energetic everythingness of space.
It is a stillness, an openness,
a putting on hold of activity
and preoccupation, this quiet,
a brief but necessary pause
between panting breaths
amid the pain and messiness of labour.

And it is not a solitary thing, our mahi.
We are surrounded by a birthing team,
a cloud of witnesses, a heavenly host
midwives, doctors-on-call, security staff
and gift shop attendants
and our whanau of shepherds and wise ones
mythmakers and storytellers,
light-bearers and road-straighteners
each with gifts and tasks,
helping us bring forth the Loving Kingdom.

We hold in our hearts this night,
families forced to seek refuge
with sometimes hostile neighbours;
those for whom a hay-filled stable would be luxury
compared with life on the street or in detention camps.

We think of those for whom the season of celebration
means stealthy escape to women's refuge
children taken into foster care, at midnight,
by strangers: police or social workers,
little ones who've never owned first-hand clothes
or a toothbrush or a book.

We think of those for whom the festive season brings
the anniversary of tragedy:
loved ones lost on the roads or at the beach,
through suicide or family violence.

We hold in our hearts those who will be alone
for the first time this year,
following death of a partner, loss of a child,
divorce or separation,
relocation to a different town or aged care unit

And we think of those struggling to resist
the thoughtless colleagues offering alcohol;
those with eating disorders, expected to over-indulge
as part of the family's tradition;
those with social anxiety
who'd rather be anywhere than at a party.

As we wait in the busy quiet,
for the birth of a new day
and the rebirth of Light
we are not alone.
We give thanks for those who went before us,
living the change, smashing glass ceilings,
loving their enemies
and speaking truth to power!

We give thanks for this gathered community
and for companions—near and far—on the star-led path
who encourage and inspire us,
rebirth and embody with us
the symbol and the Word made flesh:
manaakitanga, aroha, shalom.

Spring to summer

Prayers on the last Sunday of Spring in Aotearoa New Zealand (Optional theme: The Reign of Christ)

We give thanks for the spring which is almost at an end.
This time next week we'll be in summer and a new season
with different sorts of miracles will begin.

On this last Sunday of spring, at the approach of Advent,
let us reflect on the different insights that a new season,
a new set of experiences—or the same ones over again—
can bring.

We hold in our hearts all who need healing
of body, spirit and mind, and those who care for them.
We give thanks for all healers, professionals and volunteers,
therapists, practitioners and friends;

those who care for us, in our dark times, in our lighter times
those for whom the hardest thing to do
is realise that sometimes you can do nothing
except be there
and that may the richest gift—

A gift we all can offer:
    forgiving ourselves and others
    treading lightly, living thoughtfully
    [*optional*: celebrating the reign *or* the kindom of Christ]
    in our communities and on the sacred earth.

Suddenly there is light all around

Suddenly there is light all around
and the silences
of morning

a small town
waking
birds
distant cattle
work-bound traffic on the road outside
voices, muted and curious
laughter, footsteps

Such an ordinary light
skimming a cup
nudging the rim of a bowl
gilding one wooden arm
of an old chair
dust spangling in sunshine

The smell of grass, baled hay
and wood smoke
bread fresh from a nearby oven
earth
and blood
and new milk

And the brightness
the dizzying, commonplace brilliance of
oh! falling in love:
the universe contracts
into a blessed trinity

of elbow, breast and fontanelle.

We ask—and answer

As we anticipate the birthing-day
of the one who brings good news
who cares for the careless and the uncared for
who notices a fledgling's fall—

we think of our sisters and brothers around the world
whose lives are disrupted
—like Joseph's, like Mary's, like their extended families'—
by cultural, economic or natural disaster,
by war, terrorism, homelessness,
rejection and detention even at the borders of freedom;

we think of our sisters and brothers right here in Aotearoa
children whose lives are devastated, emotions shredded
teens dehumanised
by neglect or abuse from those who should love them
unconditionally—

and ask, what can we do?

And then we answer
        with People's Climate Marches
        by supporting refugees
        requiring that governments and banks
        divest from fossil fuels investment
        buying fairly traded goods
        and lobbying for a living wage

Living our faith
        nourishing our whānau of blood and of choice
        being family to orphans and widows
        and strangers in our midst.

Wonder of life-stories told afresh

In this season when we're urged to spend
and max out our cards and pay later
and *not* count the cost;
when many people really give until it hurts,
until there's nothing left for necessities,
until they start a new year
not in high hopes but deep in debt;

In this season where gold and frankincense
are balanced with myrrh
may we remember to share those things that have
value beyond price: a smile to a stranger,
help with heavy bags,
other random acts of kindness.

As we hear familiar stories at this time of year
may we listen as though for the first time;
let go of cynicism or boredom
and be open to the wonder of our life-stories told afresh.

In this season of giving and getting,
forgetting and remembering,
may we find wealth in generosity of spirit.
May our priority in this season be to honour life,
beginning with the life we each have and moving on
into the life that surges all around us.

Spirit of love, joy, peace and hope
despite all the challenges around the world and in our lives
we give thanks for the grace, compassion and
persistent love throughout the universe;
for the possibility and promise of transformation,
and for hope reborn each year.

Optional Response
For grace, for compassion, for the promise of transformation, for the
persistent love in all creation, we give thanks.

You who delight me

You who delight me
welcome!

You who thrill me
to aspects of myself untried:
welcome

You who enliven me
waking in me the forgotten things
the unborn things
the shadow things which unfurl and strive into light;
You who satisfy me:
welcome

You who overwhelm me
transcending words
taking my breath away:
welcome

You who entertain me
asking the foolish questions
wearing the foolish robes and silly hat
the mask and wig and jester's shoes to match my own;

You who applaud when I prance and joke
play up to me and let me be unreal
matching me jape for jest
trading me tricks for tears;
You who entertain me as I play my threadbare games:
welcome

You who transport me
from who I seem in the world of day-to-day
to who I am—unique in the universe and full of wonder
welcome

You whose star shines over this stable door
twinkling, wobbling, unstabling me
finding amongst this straw
some miracle
oiling these creaky hinges

chancing this splintering wood, these brittle barriers—
come in and welcome!

You who delight me
you who are my delight
you in whose passion the Christ-life is reborn
Welcome!

Affirmations, calls to worship & responses

Affirmation of faith for Advent

Litany with *responses in italics*

By faith, Mary let go of fear,
and engendered a mothering God.
This faith may lead us through labyrinths of doubt,
laughing hysterically, shouting in protest, lurching in denial,
finally making it to our tūrangawaewae.

By faith, Joseph took comfort from a dream
embracing complex, reconstituted,
extended family relationships.
This faith might reshape our preconceptions,
birthing new ways of being whānau.

By faith, wise ones followed the path of a new star
to a strange land, to an undistinguished stable.
This faith might sometimes lead us down unpaved tracks,
with people we don't recognise,
to destinations we didn't plan.

Faith is the opposite of belief:
a bright-side-up coin whose shadow-side is hope.

Faith is relationship and way of life
caring for orphans and widows,
casting out demons of self-doubt and despair
and occasionally raising the dead.

This is our faith:
Living as if we matter.

Living with uncertainty yet acting with confidence,
walking the star-led spiral to the heart of everything:
God in us, now—and here.

Come, let us walk the road

Come, let us walk the road that Mary walked
the challenging road
from Nazareth to Bethlehem
not knowing what the future holds.

Come, let us walk the road that Joseph walked
not sure what we are taking on
but standing to be counted
no matter the cost of such love.

Come, let us walk the road that Jesus walked
from Bethlehem – via Jerusalem – to Galilee
from Advent to Easter
from new birth to new life.

Star—Light—Word

For the Star that shone in the beginning
for the Light reborn in our hearts
for the Word embodied in us:
We give thanks.

Word made flesh in a baby

For wisdom in the Word of old
for contemporary insights in story and song
for Word made flesh in a baby—and in us
We give thanks.

Word reborn—embodied

For the Word that was in the beginning,
for the Word reborn in our hearts,
for the Word embodied in us:
We give thanks.

We crouch with Mary on the straw

We wait in the silence of a new season
moving from spring to summer
from Pentecost to Advent
from busyness to quiet.

We crouch with Mary on the straw of our messy lives
letting go of everything but this moment.
We breathe in organic and homely smells
we breathe out the impulse to push, to rush
to stock up, to plan, to get things done
—and we wait. We wait.

We listen.
It is not yet time for labour.

This is the hour of rest.
This is the time for silence, breathing,
gestation
of a nascent, quickening Christ.

Reflections

Angel messages

They didn't really have a lot to say. A bit like a singing telegram: deliver the message then fade away, attention shifting to the birthday person. The lyrics focussed, expertly drafted by a superb celestial copy writer.

And the message? Just what the hearers needed at the time; no frills, no preaching, no long-winded exhortations—just the essentials:

Don't worry! I've got great news that will make everyone happy.
The Liberator is here, in this province, this town.
This is who he's with and here's how you'll recognize him.
Praise be to God, and joy to the world.

Come to think of it, the angel messengers who appeared earlier to Mary and to Joseph didn't hang around chatting, either. In this story, at least, it seems the role of angels is to appear, reassure the audience, give a message, and challenge them to action—and then leave, to let the hearer respond as they will.

What's the angel message to you this day? Let your imagination take over for a moment; don't be afraid, still your breathing, let the music swirl around you.

Whatever form your angels take—an understanding friend, moments of indescribable transcendence, the lyrics of a popular song, spirit of nature and wilderness, your subconscious breaking through the usual thought-chatter— let your angel speak.

What do you need to hear?
The message may be very personal: *Don't be afraid.*
It could be for a general audience: *Peace on earth, goodwill to all.*
Maybe your angel message is: *You're not alone. Terrified as you are, there are other shepherds in the field with you.*

If you're the one who usually ministers to others: *Even angels have company. Awe-inspiring as we may be, even surrounded by the radiance of God's glory, there's a host of us, keeping company, harmonising, sharing the mission.*

If you're not frightened, and angel messages are nothing new; if you've often perceived messages from outside yourself or from deep within, have you shared this gift with others? Do you hug the mystery away in your heart, and feel special? Perhaps in the coming year you could show those you care for your practice of stillness and meditation, so peace can infuse them—and you can delight in their angels, too.

Could the message be: *Don't focus on the smelly cattle shed, or the bloodstained hay: look up at the star?*

"The shepherds went back to their flocks, glorifying and praising God for all they had heard and seen. It was just as the angel had told them."

Perhaps the message is: *Go on, do the thing you know is waiting, you'll be glad you did.*

When you come back—and, like the shepherds, you *will* come back to your field, to your every day, to the real world of stubborn sheep and thistly hillsides, foot rot and scabby mouth, a mother ewe rejecting one of her new-born twins, the green paddock of stumble-footed, bouncing week-old lambs, and angels and number eight wire and ozone depletion and weather forecasting—when you come back, it will be just as the angel said.

"All who heard the shepherds' story were astonished, but Mary kept all these things in her heart and thought about them often."

Mary knows now that angels come in different guises, with a different message for each person and each occasion.

With her baby in her arms and her husband by her side, with the barn full of visitors and the stock needing their manger back, the angels' message to Mary today is quite different from the message all those months ago, to a frightened teenage girl in a terrifying predicament.

She knows now that things can change, that the glory, the radiance, the sense of wonder can stay with you, to keep in your heart and call on when you need it, whatever the future brings.

Do you hear angel voices?

It's Christmas Day. The gaps between worlds are very thin today. We've come to a thin place, where angel voices might reach us more easily.

Close your eyes. Listen.

We sense the spaces between the molecules, the God-shaped gap in our rationalism, the secret and shared hopes: that this year, the perfect gift will be under the tree and dinner won't be overcooked, that family fights will be trivial, laughter will drown out disharmony, and no-one cheats at Hobbit Monopoly or refuses to share their Lego or decapitates their sister's Dora the Explorer.

These are relevant things. These are the stuff of our lives, the structure of our universe.

At Christmas, we suspend disbelief, we sing of angels and shepherds and signs and wonders and peace on earth, and for this special time, we let go of doubt and pessimism, and make space for wonder.

In this sacred space, we allow ourselves a vision of goodwill: that good blokes will take the car keys off drunk mates; that drivers won't overtake on dangerous corners; that the police and fire fighters and medical staff and undertakers might—just once—have a silent night, a new and glorious morn; that women's refuges, and men's, might be empty, and food banks full.

That the hope that's born in us today will grow and flourish in the year to come.

Can you think of a time when the angels didn't sing? When their message didn't get through? If you don't hear your angel the first time, she'll return with a vast host of others to grab your attention.

Perhaps you heard your angel long ago, but you've forgotten his song. Listen for familiar words to a different tune, or a change of tempo and different lyrics.

Maybe your angel's saying, *Get your fingers out of your ears. Don't make us blast you with ear-splitting trumpets, don't make us dance attendance 'til you think you're ready, don't dismiss us as pseudo-mysticism, don't try to balance us on a pin head or explain us away. Or—You expected this, didn't you? You know things are changing, something needs your attention. There's a new life waiting, a miracle only you can make happen.*

If you ignore her in the fields, this time she'll ambush you in the street. If choral music doesn't grab you, perhaps a reggae beat or neon sign or bumper sticker will bring good news. Even if you don't believe in angels, listen to them sing!

Today, throughout the holiday season, and in the New Year, listen for the message from your angel:

Hear my song.
Let my strong wings enfold you.

But where are the others?

While Mary and Joseph bump along the Bethlehem Road on donkey back, and settle into temporary accommodation in the downstairs room where the feed's stored and the domestic animals come for milking, do you ever wonder where Joseph's other children are?

In all the *dramatis personae* of the nativity scene, with angels and shepherds and wise ones from afar, no-one mentions the half-brothers and sisters in Nazareth.

While the inn-keeper's wife and her sisters and the midwife bustle around and lay clean sheets on the straw mattress and tell Joseph to go boil some water, and call their daughters to bring fortified wine and vinegar-water and a clean pottery bowl for the afterbirth;

while the men pace the market, chewing dates and offering Joseph a swig from a wineskin they think's a secret from their wives, and brag about their sons and their prowess;

does Joseph remind them he's already a father? That this is not his first time pacing and drinking and joking with brothers-in-law and cousins?

Does he hope, especially here, in his hometown, the city of his ancestor David—with an intensity that shames him, that he'd *never* even hint at to Mary—that he's seen as man enough to father a son?

When Joseph overhears the panting and straining, when Mary's sobs and groans are almost more than he can bear, does he think of that other woman, the mother of children whose births he wasn't there for?

And when tears well in his eyes at the lusty cry of his tiny son, is he remembering and perhaps still grieving for his first wife, for the children re-housed with relatives, missing their mother, missing their father more because they see him from time to time? Does he worry that the boys won't get on, that this newest one—whose conception and paternity is gossiped about by the fostering aunts—might not be welcomed by his first family?

And once they're back in Nazareth, as the young Mary watches her boy growing in wisdom and stature, does she strive, with a perception beyond her years, to involve them in the new family she and Joseph are forming, to nurture their inquisitive interest in their half-brother, to make them feel as loved and as special as he is?

Does Mary foresee that his story, his purpose, will be carried into the future by his half-brothers, by Joseph's other sons?

This liturgical year [2016], St Andrew's Day coincided with the first Sunday in Advent, and we were reminded of Andrew, the quiet disciple, the younger brother overshadowed by boisterous Simon Peter.

Andrew was an observer, a doer. When asked where he lived, his reply was a simple, "Come and see."

Of all Jesus' followers, Andrew understood manaakitanga, welcome, sharing. His attitude was not, *What do you believe, whose side are you on*, but *Make yourself at home. All are welcome here*.

We try to live that way, too—even if it means being at odds with some of our church family, even if it means being prepared to defy some decisions of our national organisation.

Sometimes, Jesus' family thought he was going too far. His mother and brothers tried to get him to tone it down, keep the discussion pleasant and not disturb the peace. They said, "Are you out of your mind? Come home, and calm down a bit."

And his response? "A prophet's not respected in his own home!" With even more hyperbole, "You have to hate your parents and desert your family to follow me!"

Shocking, isn't it? Like saying the rich won't get into heaven, or don't waste your pearls of wisdom on these swine. Like turning the tables in the temple and shouting, "You've made the economy more important than human lives!"

It's not comfortable, looking forward from the Bethlehem manger to the streets of Jerusalem, the shores of Galilee, the pubs and whorehouses of Nazareth, the badlands of Samaria. Yet, that's where Jesus found his friends and followers, and in a few years' time, that's where we'll find him.

But, for now, let the future be as it will, and let's focus once more on the family at the heart of our story. And look, we're not alone! Others feel as we do, accepting the challenge to "Come and see."

As we gather around the child of hope, we're joined by a heavenly host. The kindom of heaven gathers with us—

But where are the others? The brothers and sisters, the half-brothers and step-sisters, the broken relations, torn-apart siblings, the unblended families, the reconstituted ones.

All the children with bruises on their bodies; fathers with bruises on their psyches; mothers with bruises on their hearts.

Here they are! The jailbird cousin and the crazy aunt. The depressed daughter who's dragged herself out; the edge-of-hysteria, manic sister; the autistic grandson behind a haybale, rocking; the transgendered, the cisgendered, the queer and the straight, the birth children and adopted children and fostered children; these fragile families of blood and of choice.

All the whānau of Jesus: gathered to celebrate heaven on earth, in the promise of a child.

And in the lower room, with Mary and Joseph and baby Jesus, are brothers Simon and Jude, Joses and James, and the unnamed sisters. There's Anne and Joachim, and Joseph's misidentified parents; Elizabeth, Zacharias and cousin John; the whole extended, overwhelmed and slowly healing family of God.

And here we are, in our tattered rags and party clothes. Whispering or shouting: Love is here! In our land, our city, our home.

The news—too good not to share—shines in our eyes: every life is precious, every gift has worth, every day, we can give birth to hope.

Come, says Andrew. Come and see.

Come, says Jesus, come follow me—

and year after year, this ordinary miracle draws us together, midwives of change, guests at the feast.

This is our story: familiar, sometimes taken for granted, yet each year resounding new.

So, for the two thousand and umpteenth time: Shalom! Happy Christmas!

Today and every day until we meet again around the manger:

Peace be with you! Joy to the world! Love is born again.

Doors wide open

"Like the warmth of the summer wind you come"—

Mark Wilson's "**You are born in us again**" is one of my favourite Christmas Carols and inspired this reflection for Christmas Eve. You can find it in the NZ Hymnbook Trust's **Carol Our Christmas**

Picture this: A small house, in a close-knit community; the sounds of hammering and a plane scraping across wood, and men's voices— husband, stepsons—as they work; the smells of baking and lamb roasting.

A young, tired woman bustling around the kitchen, setting the table, glancing out the window at the afternoon shadows, neighbours gossiping in the street, sideways glances. The feeling of still being under suspicion, not quite fitting in, even with things going well—so far.

And just when there's still so much to do, the sound of little feet hurrying up the steps, and that dear, persistent, interrupting young voice: "Mama, where did I come from?"

"Not now, Jesus," says his mother. "I'm busy. Go outside and play, there's a good boy."

"But Mama, I don't like it outside just now. It's too windy. The wind blows sand in my eyes. Where does…?"

"Go and help your big brothers, then; they might let you help tidy the workbench before the Sabbath. Or Abba Joseph might want you to help polish that new cabinet he's been making."

"But Mama, where does the wind come from?" Mary gives a little sigh, and sits down to polish the glasses, carefully putting each one at its place on the table, and tries to answer her son.

"Little philosopher, who knows? The wind blows wherever it wants to. You can't tell where it comes from, or where it's going. But you know it's there, don't you?"

A puzzled frown, more questions in those big brown eyes.

"You can feel it on your face; you can feel the wind ruffling your hair—like this!" A tender, work-worn hand rests briefly on the precious head.

He ducks, and pulls away. "But why, Mama? Why does the wind tickle like that?" "Pass me the fruit sauce in that dish—carefully! Good boy, put it in the middle of the table, there. Well, the wind is like your breath, isn't it, like your spirit. You need the air to breathe, and the wind is like a great big breath—puffing at you, hurrying you along the road when you're dawdling..."

"Past the soldiers, Mama."

"Yes, son, past the soldiers—quickly. If it's a nice warm wind it makes you feel good, though, makes you want to dance in it. You remember, when we went to visit Aunt Eliza and Uncle Zach in Judea, how you little ones ran about in the wind?"

"We're not little, Mama, we're big boys now. I'm nearly as big as John, aren't I? I'm nearly as old as he is, aren't I Mama?"

"Only a few months, yes; he's just a bit older than you are."

"He always wants to go in front of me, though. Why won't he let me go first, sometimes? What's your spirit, mama?"

"Listen, Jesus, you should be grateful for your cousin going ahead of you. He smooths things for you sometimes, doesn't he? Introduces you to his friends? 'This is my cousin, Jesus,' he says. 'He's my special friend.' He even helps you tie the thongs of your sandals!"

"He eats locusts! Ugh!" says the small boy, Jesus, screwing up his mouth and wrinkling his sun-freckled nose. "And he's always paddling about in the river, splashing people! Getting me all wet."

"Yes, but he shares the wild honey with you, doesn't he, and shows you the best places to go fishing? And he gave you his spare tunic, didn't he? Oh, that's the door banging! Did you leave it open again? Anyone would think you were born in a stable!"

"It's just the wind blowing the door open. It's good to have the door open, so your friends can come in. Mama, look, here's Abba!"

"Joseph, good! You tell your son what the wind is! I've got to check the lamb, and pour the wine—and the sun's getting low in the sky. Go on, go 37 with your father and stop asking questions, always questions. Enough already!"

"Daddy, Abba, do you like the wind? Mama doesn't know where it comes from. Do you know? She says I was born in a stable. Was I really? What's the wind, Abba?"

"Well, son, the wind comes to blow away the cobwebs and dust and the wood shavings that make the floor messy. You come with me, and give Mary some peace for a bit; she's got a lot to do today.

"The wind, now, it freshens things up. On a very, very hot day it's good to feel a cool breeze, isn't it? Like a wash in the river when you're tired and dusty, or like a hug when you're feeling grumpy or scared or sad."

"Abba Joseph, is it like love? The wind. Is it like when you let me have a little candle near my bed coz of the dark, and you leave the door open so I can hear you in the workshop?"

"Clever little chap—you'll maybe be a Rabbi or even a Pharisee one day, if you don't fancy the carpenter's shop... and I can't see you being happy there, indoors all day, making crosses for the wretched Romans and taking commissions for their empire-building! But enough of them. I suppose they bring us business."

"What's crosses for, Abba? Do we have to love the Romans? You said I should try and love everybody. I saw some soldiers today! Why's love like the wind, Abba? Tell me again!"

"Such things you ask, boy! Yes, the wind is like love—sometimes. You can't see it but you can feel it, and you don't always know where it comes from, but suddenly it's there, pushing you off course, carrying you away!"

"I don't understand! Mama says it makes you want to dance. But she was cross when the door banged!"

"Well, that's just it. Suddenly the door's open—like your heart. Things peaceful for a bit, then, whoosh! It's like being born again, into a world where everything's bigger, and good, and right. Good, here are your brothers. Now, let's dance back inside and you can help Mama light the candles. It's almost time."

A wry glance at this precocious, sweet-tempered child; this surprise in his middle age; this love-child of such mystery and ordinariness.

"Jesus, you help Mama carry the herbs and salt to the table, that's a good lad; she's been working so hard all day, taking care of you, answering questions, getting this special meal ready," says the pragmatic Joseph.

"Mary, come and sit down now. You've been rushing around like the wind all day. Ah, this so good! Our family, good food, wine from new wine skins. If God had only given us the Sabbath, that would have been enough! And here's our little lad, growing up fine and strong, like his brothers."

"And questions, always the questions, and asking for stories!" says Mary. "I'm sure he's nearly ready for temple school. James, prop the door open, for Elijah, that's right! Now, son, this is the time to ask your questions; you know what you have to say?"

And the boy Jesus sits up straight at the table, with its smooth surface and straight legs, and the clean cloth and the dishes of lamb and rosemary, the water and the salt, and the empty wine glass—and he begins, "Why is this night different from all other nights?"

And each year, all around the world, wherever we gather together to share bread and wine, at Passover, at Christmas, at Hanukkah, at Easter, we ask—"Will it be born in us again? The love, the compassion, the commonwealth of peace and freedom?"

And each year anew, the answer comes: the hope, the promise and fulfilment—blowing the doors wide open, like a summer wind; opening our hearts.

Gifts for a baptism

New Year reflection for Epiphany and the Baptism of Jesus

By the time the wise ones get to Bethlehem—or it is Nazareth by now?— the baby who, this time last year was gurgling angelically in the manger and waving his little toes, has discovered how to climb on a footstool and open the knife drawer.

By now he's able to reach the shelf with the Shabbat candles and the precious Torah scroll; he's having great fun with the wood-shavings in Joseph's carpenter's shed, and trying to taste the nails and bang things with a hammer.

Whoever they are and wherever they come from, the Magi won't be gathered romantically around a manger, with picturesquely mooing cows and lullaby-baaing sheep. The precious gifts would probably have been abandoned in favour of the packaging. And any sweet-smelling hay would be composting with the Middle Eastern version of dirty nappies and wet wipes.

And Mary, no longer with beautiful blue draperies and Madonna smile, is preparing meals for Joseph and her step-sons, keeping an eye on the toddler Jesus, negotiating kitchen space with a disapproving mother-in-law and trying to ignore the gossip still circulating in his extended family. (Joseph might have married her and named the child, but they still refer to Jesus as *the son of Mary*.)

And yet—wise ones sought him.

When preparing this service, not sure how today's themes of Epiphany and the Baptism of Jesus, years later, could be interwoven, I was pleased to find this hymn whose words were written around 450 CE, linking Jesus' birth, the magi's visit, his baptism in the Jordan, the miracle at Cana and the season of Epiphany: *[listen to or sing]* "The Star Proclaims the King Is Here."

And still, around the world, we picture the homely stable and the exotic kings, the exhausted young mother and the noble stepfather, giving and taking meaning and reinterpreting the stories in our ways, for our times and places.

Perhaps the early artists got the spirit right, with their crowded nativity scenes: Magi and shepherds and family and neighbours, patrons and village gossips, merchants and royalty, creatures great and small, human and animal, all gathering in wonder at the miracle and promise of the new-born.

The season of Epiphany in the liturgical calendar is designated "ordinary time." After a month-long build-up in Advent, all anticipation and preparation, we spend Christmas Eve and Christmas Day celebrating Jesus' birth and then it's pretty much all over.

On the first Sunday in the New Year we celebrate the visit of the mysterious wise ones from the East, and by the 12th of January or thereabouts, we're skipping ahead some 30 years to celebrate Jesus' baptism, as an adult, by his cousin the famous preacher, teacher and somewhat eccentric prophet, John.

We understand that Jesus, as a baby, was "dedicated" at the synagogue; the back story of his being recognised by ancient Simeon and Anna keeps us on track with how special he was. And at age 12 the boy genius engages in discussion with the temple scholars for days until his parents realise he's not with the extended family travelling home from Passover in Jerusalem. We can imagine some unholy words when they find him, and the profuse apologies to the temple scholars and rabbis for their precocious son's behaviour.

And then we lose track of the boy and the teenage Jesus—and perhaps it's just as well, because not too many holy ones could stand up to scrutiny through the years of wilfulness and silences and experimenting with the dregs from old wine skins; claiming he's with his cousin, when in fact he's out with his gang, his home boys, following the Roman soldiers, chasing the neighbours' chickens and taunting the billy goat; leaving the sheepfold gate open. We miss the door slamming and "You just don't understand!" and "Anyway you're not my *real* father!"

And suddenly here he is, the carpenter's son, being a *hackhem,* a wise guy, in temple; reading and preaching as if he knows better than the rabbis who've interpreted Torah for years, for decades! Partying in Cana and somehow producing more wine when the embarrassed hosts of the wedding can't find the supplies they've been stocking up on since the betrothal.

Can't you hear the gossip?

He's been hanging out with some unsavoury people—tax collectors and girls who're no better than they should be (just like his mother, some would say); going off with the fishers or hanging around the religious zealots; insisting they're just people, even the Samaritans— and he didn't meet them in *our village!—and taking risks among lepers and the moon-struck and demon-possessed.*

First it was foreigners with their camels and gold and exotic spices when he was small; and next he's bringing home lame ducks and lost causes, and expecting them all to be welcomed; to be treated normally, like family from another village perhaps—not special guests, just ordinary, he says.

And now, he's up north with his cousin John, clever John, who arrived in almost as miraculous a way—conceived by a mother well past childbearing age, just like Abraham and Sarah, and his father struck dumb.

In the temple, yet. And him a priest, what will they think of your son, the radical, the wilderness man, with his fasting and praying and preaching and baptising.

And his mother's reply: *And yet they come to him from miles around, wanting to hear his theories; he can pull a crowd, my Yochanan! But he should keep out of politics. He shouldn't upset the rulers or call attention to himself!*

We skip so quickly from the birth of Jesus to the Ordinary, from Advent to Lent & Passiontide, often forgetting we're still in the season of "revelation" or "manifestation", of sudden appearances and wonder and the sharing of gifts of the spirit, of wisdom and healing and hospitality, and star-led journeys.

The birth, epiphany and baptism stories all feature people travelling significant distances to find meaning, to acknowledge someone special, and to give or receive extraordinary gifts:

Mary and Joseph with their trusty if fictitious donkey, travelling from Nazareth to Bethlehem, and the precious gift of a baby whose story would impact millions of lives for over two thousand years.

Wise ones travelling from afar to worship—literally, to bow and show respect—to a special little one, guided by heavenly bodies, bringing gifts with spiritual and royal significance. Jesus' own journey to the Jordan River for baptism, and the gift of the dove-shaped spirit, and the mysterious Voice of God expressing approval.

And all this leads, through twists and turns as stories and celebrations and symbols do, to our giving gifts at a child's christening or baptism, and at Christmas, and in annual celebration of each other's miraculous birth—and in our gathering to tell and retell the stories of our faith.

What gifts can we continue to share this season? What journeys are still to be made?

May the love we share at Christmas and the wonder of Epiphany stay and inspire us, so we can recognise in every human being, a precious God-child and Gift.

Holy Families—outrageous possibilities

"Hope starts small, even as a seed in the womb, but it feeds on outrageous possibilities."—Jan Richardson, Night Visions

Imagine you've been sitting on the hillside, minding your sheep and your own business, when suddenly the angelic host appears and frightens you out of your wits. Then fast forward a bit—you're running towards Bethlehem to see the new baby and his family.

Now, freeze frame again:

How do you see the Holy Family? What do they look like? "Ordinary"?— what does that mean? Iconic? A nativity scene or an artist's impression? Surrounded by shepherds and angels and animals, or isolated and on the run from Herod—or from dubious family members still unsure of Joseph's wisdom in marrying Mary? Perhaps you see a pageant—a filmstrip of images one after the other, screening numerous family scenes and mythologies and narratives. Hold them in your mind's eye.

In a young adult book by Terry Pratchett, young Johnny— dysfunctional family, odd friends, approaching adolescence—finds himself in a computer game that's become real. From the blurb: "Johnny Maxwell, 12, thinks he's a loser. People don't seem to notice him, his parents are threatening to split up, and he's not very good at the shoot-up-the-bad-guys computer games that he and his friends are always playing. But after his hacker buddy, Wobbler, gives him an illegal copy of *Only You Can Save Mankind*, strange things happen." Johnny's battling aliens, and finds he has to be a hero, a saviour; he has to make the right decisions. In fact, "Johnny... has to learn how to wage all-out Peace."

The book poses the question, "If Not You, Who Else?" Johnny finds out that, with a bit of help, he can in fact save mankind. It's fantasy. It has the kind of ending that's—well, it's hopeful.

A young woman, betrothed as was customary but not yet married, complex social relationships, the invasion of alien ideas—dreams— visitations, an unplanned pregnancy, unexpected responsibilities at an early age. Mary finds she's giving birth to a hero, a saviour; she and Joseph must make the right decisions. In fact, their child will come to be called the Prince of Peace. It's mythical. It has a kind of hopeful ending.

"Hope starts small, even as a seed in the womb, but it feeds on outrageous possibilities."

And today's story? Our holy families. Outrageous possibilities suggested, challenges set before us, dreams and visions of what might be. On Christmas Eve, we come to be re-inspired, to seek the mystery, to find answers in a stable, hope in a cattle shed.

This Advent we've been challenged by the Christian World Service, whose theme for this year [2013] is, "Save the Earth; Save its Peoples". It can be frightening. The Christian World Service "angels" can overwhelm us with how much there is to be done, but they've also shared stories of what people and groups are doing around the world, and what we can do, here in Aotearoa New Zealand.

Marian Wright Edelman knows about possibilities. Marian's a lawyer, educator, activist, and the first African American woman admitted to the Mississippi state bar. This is what she has to say—and I've added Jesus to the heroes she names: "It's time for greatness—not for greed. It's a time for idealism—not ideology. It is a time not just for compassionate words, but compassionate action... A lot of people are waiting for Martin Luther King or Mahatma Gandhi [or Jesus] to come back—but they are gone. We are it. It is up to us. It is up to you."

So, for a moment, re-run the film; sit still on the hillside once more, as the angels appear—and this time, try not to be frightened because they're giving us a clue: Peace and Goodwill, that's how we save the earth. When hope and joy, peace and love are born in us, and influence what we do.

This year, next year, it's our families who need to be the holy families, the communities of possibility and hope. This year, next year—day by day, in the attitudes we hold, the decisions we make, we can save the earth, and save its peoples. Not through grand gestures and heroic deeds, but through storytelling and nurturing the hope, stepping out with sometimes inexplicable faith, celebrating the outrageous possibility that our gifts are already changing the world, saving humankind, saving the earth.

For example: through schemes like the one where you get a tag from the Birthright Christmas tree, and buy a gift for the named child. So Leilani aged 12 who might not otherwise have received a Christmas present, will get something from Santa that cost under $30.00 and took less than 10 minutes to choose.

Or by supporting organisations whose focus is on child welfare and parenting—Plunket, Barnardos, Birthright, Family Planning, UNICEF—most of whom make saving the world so easy online or by phone—just click to make a donation, or text to donate.

Waging all-out Peace. If not us, who else?

Fast forward again!

Down off the hillside—angels carolling encouragement, the three wise queens running by our sides with their food bank trolleys, our friends and neighbours wanting to share the good news, the star racing through the heavens, arriving in tandem as we reach the stable door, shining its image of hope and wonder.

Shining over us and the family and the animals, the lowing cattle, the braying donkey, the silly sheep; the earth in all its fullness spinning with us, tumbling down the hillside, skidding up to the familiar scene—where an outrageous family, an ordinary family, a holy family, a world of outrageous possibilities lies swaddled in Christmas wrapping, tugging at our hearts.

This year, next year—outrageous possibilities are at our fingertips, in our hands.

If not now, when will we save the earth?

If we don't save its people, who will?

I have to differ

This reflection is an extract, slightly adapted, from an assignment *Manna from Heaven: Is demythologization helpful in understanding the miracles of the Bible?* which I wrote in January 2000 for a Religious Studies paper at Victoria University of Wellington

Miracles no longer miraculous?

In his New Testament and Mythology, Bultmann claims that "modern man is convinced that the mythical view of the world is obsolete", that "all our thinking today is shaped for good and ill by modern science", "the miracles of the new testament have ceased to be miraculous", and— astonishingly—that "the mythical view of the world must be accepted or rejected in its entirety."

I have to differ!

As I do my Christmas shopping and decorate my tree with a plastic angel and fake snow, I know that Santa Claus and his elves are busy working away in the North Pole: I may not *believe* it rationally, but it has become part of my "story" so that demythologizing it would destroy the magical experience which, each year, I choose to enter.

Demythologizing and Mozart

In January, after a festive break reading trashy novels, I struggled through readings for a university Religious Studies paper. While reading Bultmann's essay on demythologizing scripture, I listened to Mozart's *Great Mass in C Minor*.

Rationally, literally, I do not *believe in* an external transcendent God.

Yet when Herbert von Karajan conducts the Berliner Philharmoniker in the adagio "Jesu Christe" or "Cum Sancto Spirito," how could I respond—how can any of us respond—except to join in: "Amen, Amen"?

Kissing the face of God

Every year, in manses and studies and at the kitchen table, preachers and worship leaders approach Advent with a mixture of joy and trepidation.

Joy, because Christmas is the penultimate Christian festival—each week the excitement builds, every week another candle is lit, every year is pregnant with possibilities—but trepidation, because December 25 after December 25, the person leading the service tries to find something new to say!

Because we're quite impatient these days, with repetition and slogans and the same old, same old. And we want something real: not some facsimile of Christmas with tinsel branches and limping reindeer; we want the genuine smell of *pinus radiata* and a champagne breakfast, no last minute defrosted turkey or re-gifted tins of biscuits!

We want the genuine article, the perfect gift: a *real* Christmas.

We might wrap our presents in brown paper and cotton twine, as if this costs the environment less than glossy a Santa and curling ribbon, but we sneak an envious glance at adverts where someone unwraps several layers of hand-printed paper and finds, nestled in tissue, that perfect thing:

proof that this year someone cared enough to choose it and write our name on the label; evidence that someone loves us. In the words of the fabulous advertising campaign— that, even while we're mocking it, makes us smile—because *we're worth it!*

On Christmas morning when the beach is calling, and the family's gathering and the presents are a mystery (or feel book-shaped!), and after the splendour and celebration of Christmas Eve, we don't want Christmas Day to be an anti-climax.

We've gifted our Oxfam goats or ducks and bought our Conservation diaries, and what we'd like, on Christmas Day, what we really want, is for things to be—perfect. Just like the old days.

Something new, but also something familiar.

And that's what's so wonderful about the Christmas story, and why preachers penning their reflections approach with trepidation but also with joy: at Christmas, the news is all good.

Year after year, the traditional is transformed. There's been drama and scandal and mystery but finally the child's delivered safely. Over years, decades, centuries, the story evolves and grows, twists like a streamer and shines along a new star path.

And at its very heart is the thing we want, we need, to hear:

You are loved. You are worthy. Your life is the most precious thing. You deserve the best: God's Child, offspring of deity, Wisdom become flesh, creation personified through an act of loving generosity.

In our wisdom readings, Dorothy Parker's poem *Prayer for a New Mother* assumes that Mary knew the things that would come later, and poignantly wishes that—for this day at least—she can spend time with her little one, un-shadowed by future events.

And in the contemporary carol, we hear that amazing question: Mary, did you know... *when you kiss your little baby you've kissed the face of God?*

What does it mean for us, to kiss the face of God?

Perhaps it's to hear Sophia, Wisdom of Creation, now in flesh appearing and to see God in the face of friend and stranger. To hear the angel song that lifts our hearts and makes us wonder how we ever could have forgotten. To hold in our arms, in imagination, that newborn and sense the hurts we absorb from one another, the grudges we hold, the wounded feelings we nurse, washed away by a wave of love we can't describe and barely comprehend. To feel our dreams born alive, held in hope, wrapped in love. To unite with friends and lovers for peace, and joy and love. Perhaps kissing the face of God is to walk lightly on the earth, to leave only footprints.

When we live with respect for our earth mother Papatūānuku and our sky father Ranginui; share the planet selflessly with all the creatures of forest, sky and sea; respect the atua of river and mountain and city street; when we share breath with other creatures of the earth, and hongi each other— maybe then, with Mary, we kiss the face of God.

Today the Christ is born again, in your manger, under your Christmas tree. Love comes gift-wrapped, hope shines over your garage door, peace is shared at your meal.

And in this shining hour, with this gleaming assurance, we can take a moment to reflect on those other days, the other mornings; the story that features not swaddling cloth but a shroud; the journey that leads through shadow lands, unhappy endings and loveless evenings, and hope exploding like methane in a coal mine.

We pause and recognise that today's message is really just scene-setting, the set-up shot for the story of a life that ends not in a birth but a shameful, traitor's death; to betrayal by friends and mocking by the indifferent. No gold or frankincense, but myrrh and vinegar and bitter aloe.

The story that leads from Bethlehem to Golgotha; from singing seraphs and startled shepherds, to the place of the skull.

In the silence, a baby cries, a bird sings, and we remember—it doesn't end there. Just as Christmas doesn't end in Bethlehem, the Easter story doesn't end in a borrowed gravesite: it goes on, through the garden and the upper room, to Galilee.

And suddenly angels are singing again, and the star of Bethlehem is shining. Herod is outwitted by wise ones, farmers move their flocks to grassy fields. And near the sea, the fisher women are also giving birth, to babies who will one day form a community around this child we celebrate; a company that will tell and retell their stories, adding a postscript here, a simile there, a metaphor for the reality of their lives.

Already a group is forming, of fishermen and tax assessors and political hopefuls, adulterers and lepers, the blind and the bleeding, the overworked and those bedevilled by illness, the rent boys and the zealots. But also, as the story grows, the healed and respected and released, Pharisees and lawyers, the sellers of purple and Ethiopian diplomats, the Corinthians, Ephesians, Mesopotamians— all, all gathered around a table that's groaning with veges and stuffing and gravy, pavlova and fruitcake, muscatels, strawberries, bubbly; fishes and loaves enough for all.

And at its heart—the heart of this band of followers, the heart of the story, the heart of our deepest desire—is the gift that's waiting for us every day: demanding, hungry, restless, embodied love.

Love that cries from its manger, that's inextricably bound with justice.

Love that humbles and inspires and compels us to care for the earth and its people, to feed its hungry and calm its seas.

Love that transcends its sometimes dubious beginnings.

Love transcending emotion, translated into action.

Love that yearns to be cradled close; to be kissed on its grubby, tearstained cheek; the most demanding and rewarding gift of all.

This is the Christmas message; the reason we come back to hear it year after year, the words Mary treasured in her heart:

You are worthy.
You are the one to birth a miracle.
You are the gift that needs no label.
You are recipient and giver of this huge, indiscriminate love.
Yours is the face that is kissed by God.

This is our story: familiar, sometimes forgotten or taken for granted, and each year sounding new. So, for the two thousand and umpteenth time:
Shalom! Happy Christmas!

Today and every day until we meet again around the manger:

Peace be with you!
Joy to the world!
Love is born again.

Today, and every day, may you kiss the face of God.
So may it be.

Mary full of grace—Anna's story

She was always a good girl, my Mary. Kind, modest, virtuous.

In a society like ours, where the men think they have a direct line to God, we women have to stick together. And in a shared household, there are women of all generations, telling stories, nudging and joking, sharing the knowing glances and—you know how it is— speaking a language peculiar to us. The one with as many gaps as sentences, the one that drives the men wild because they think we're gossiping about *them. Comparing notes,* as it were. They're so fragile, underneath the bluster. And of course, sometimes they're right, though we don't let on.

Mary rarely joins in. She's not prudish, doesn't find the eyebrow-raising stories of marriage and love-making distasteful. She's not upset when the aunties and cousins regale each other with details of their pregnancies, and compete for the dubious honour of the worst morning sickness, the most swollen ankles. When they whisper about near-impossible lovemaking positions to accommodate a husband's incomprehensible desire when you're eight months gone; or tell their most gruesome childbirth and difficult breast-feeding stories.

She listens, I assume she learns—but somehow Mary keeps herself a little apart from it all. She'll blush if anyone asks which young man she favours, and shies away from boys' obvious interest in her, young as she is. (She's a well-developed girl, comely, as the old ones used to say.)

Often as not, when I've thought she *must* be absorbing the facts of life from her older cousins, she's got her nose stuck in a book and seems oblivious to the talk all around her. I should have had one of those special mother-and-daughter talks, but I truly thought she was less—naïve.

Perhaps it's because Joachim and I weren't so young when we had her. Nothing so dramatic as Elizabeth's startlingly late pregnancy, so unlikely that her Zacharias was struck dumb! Literally, I mean. He's only recovered the power of speech since their John was born—though he never did have much to say for himself. I guess my kinswoman likes the strong and silent type.

The other thing about living communally is we're familiar with each other's moon cycles, many of us having our times of uncleanness together. That's why it's odd I didn't work out what was going on with my girl for so long; usually that sort of secret's impossible to keep. The first hint of a young woman being off her food and a bit seedy looking in the mornings, or later, blooming and ripening, and it's all significant looks and speculation.

Anyway, there it is. A few months ago, she finds me alone—which doesn't happen often—and tells me something strange and rather frightening's happened. Of course, I panicked at first; for all our talk and independence, women generally have to do as men tell us, and while the laws of Moses and our faith have severe punishments for rape, there are more subtle ways of coercing a woman. And not all our men, virtuous as they may seem, have the patience of Job or the devotion of my Joachim.

So, my little girl, our Mary, is expecting. It's not as uncommon as you'd think, and she is betrothed—in an informal way—to Joseph the artisan woodworker, but he's so much older. I thought she might be attracted to a boy her own age and this attachment mightn't last, but she seems to find him safe. He's a good man, Joseph; and she's a fine girl, so I guess it'll all work out. Despite the gossip, those bitches in the marketplace counting backwards and hinting she must have fallen while Joseph was away, selling his wood and metal wares and taking commissions.

I must say, Mary's never looked healthier, and she seems to have more self-confidence. It's as if she's got an inner light, and although she still claims not to know how it happened, being pregnant seems to agree with her. She's going around, singing, yet.

And I'm going to be a grandmother! I wonder what she'll name him...

Mary to Elizabeth

Circa 4 BCE

Letter (1)

Shalom, Elizabeth. Peace be on you and your house.

The big news—which you and Cousin Zacharias might not have heard yet— is that at last the contract has been signed on my betrothal to Joseph, son of Jacob and grandson of Matthan (of the line of King David).

You can imagine mother and her cronies! Instead of looking to the shadows on the synagogue wall, the villagers have been telling the time by mother's daily stride to the house of the matchmaker.

Meantime Jacob and my father and the other men sit under a tree, munching on dates and olives, laughing at the antics of the women. After all, a marriage between our family and Jacob's has been expected ever since father sired daughters and Jacob produced all those sons.

Jacob is a fine man with a twinkle in his eye and a kind smile, even for servants and girls. I hope his son Joseph will also be pleasant. They say is he a just man and always does what is right.

It will be strange moving into a household with so few women for company, 'though as you know I've never much minded being on my own. Now I am betrothed I must try not to wander off into the countryside, "dreaming and romancing" as mother says. I am to become one of the wives, keeping indoors and conducting myself with the reserve of a virtuous woman.

Cousin Elizabeth, can you imagine me turning into a housewife? My weaving is atrocious, my stitching is still unsteady and I even spill the grain when grinding flour. I will miss my walks, looking at the flowers in the fields and the birds of the air. I envy them sometimes! They don't have to toil and spin and gather the harvest.

I'll miss my brother, Nathan, when I go to Joseph's household. Nathan's usually nice to me and sometimes even defended me against mother's scolding. He's getting impatient, though, and wishes for action. Sometimes he talks of Moses leading our people out of Egypt, and of a Messiah coming to deliver us from the oppressors. When he's very agitated, he talks of Simon Zealotes and the band of "zealots" who still gather and plot.

I told him The Deliverer won't be among those crazy rebels; he'll come from David's line, which that Simon most certainly did not. Nathan just laughs and says Joseph is a true descendant, so who knows but the Deliverer could come from our family! As if the saviour of our people would be born of common folk like us.

A few times, Nathan has talked to me about Joseph. He thinks I should know something of the man I'm betrothed to. He says Joseph is a just man and honours the law, but isn't a "fanatical stickler." That makes Nathan admire him. He says Joseph actually offered to carry the pack of a soldier an extra mile recently, as he was travelling to deliver some goods for Jacob. Imagine doing more than you must for the Romans! But Joseph said you should be merciful to others if you want to receive mercy, and the soldier was young and recently hurt in battle.

Nathan says I should fare well with Joseph, as he's a dreamer like me. I hope he is kind as well as just. I think kindness would be a good thing in a husband, don't you, Cousin Elizabeth? Some men don't seem to honour their wives at all. It's rather frightening.

And—I have to tell someone—Nathan says Joseph has seen me in the village and going to the well, and said he thought I was very beautiful. Imagine that! No-one has ever said such a thing of me before. Do you think I'm very vain to be pleased about it?

The wedding won't take place for some time, but already mother is bustling around, making preparations and getting the whole village involved. She's boasting about the fine match she's made, and ordering barrels of figs and skins of wine, and planning what I should wear.

She says with all Jacob's boys, and Joseph's, we should produce many strong sons to carry on the families' work. I'm sorry if it grieves you for me to say this, dearest Elizabeth, but I do hope God will send me and Joseph a large family, if he wills it.

You know he's a widower, although not too old! I didn't know his first wife; she was always so busy, and pregnant with all those boys in a short time, and then she was taken, in her last childbirth, and the little one too. So he's known marriage and babies before, which is comforting but also a bit scary.

I want to be a good and honourable wife, and do what is right. Mother says being married will cure me of my waywardness and imagination. She says I won't have time for a lot of foolish nonsense. This betrothal to Joseph has pleased her a great deal. I'm a bit frightened, and can only hope he's as good a man as they say.

Mother's calling me—I must go. Shalom, dear Cousin. I hope you will be able to attend my marriage celebration, if Zacharias can get away from his temple duties for a while.

Your obedient (secretly beautiful!) cousin,
Mary

Letter (2)

Cousin Elizabeth, such a terrible thing has happened, I can't think how to tell you but you're the only one I *can* tell. I will just have to say it, and pray you won't despise me. It seems that I am with child.

How can I be with child, Cousin Elizabeth? I can only think God must have sent me a child, even though I am not yet married. Perhaps God heard me thinking of having sons with Joseph to bring honour and prosperity to both families, and sent an angel to me with a child. But the old ones say there's more to it than that, and that I've brought shame and disgrace on them all, and on Joseph too. Truly, I never wished for God to send me a child until after the marriage.

For a while I thought the sickness was because of a terrible thing that happened to me. I was alone one evening—I'll never wander off by myself again—and this person, I guess I should say "man" (I couldn't see clearly and was so afraid) appeared in front of me, and...

I can't tell you what happened, it was so terrifying. I must have fainted, because after a while I woke feeling very strange and, I don't know how to describe it, sort of *invaded*, and scared half to death.

But I got myself home without being noticed, and it was not long after that I started feeling ill and tired a lot of the time.

But at least I don't feel sick any more. I wish I could run away, but where could I go? Cousin, I really need to see you! Can I come and stay for a few moons?

In haste,
Mary

Postscript (a few days later)

I have to add this, cousin! I still don't understand what's happening, but I think everything might be all right.

Nathan told me Jacob and Joseph and his brothers came to speak to my father a couple of days ago. He says he doesn't know if Joseph's a saint or a mad man, but he's certainly going the second mile without being asked. He said both fathers were quoting the law and the prophets and shouting about shame and tradition and divorce. And in the middle of all this, Joseph stood up to them and said he was going to marry me!

But just imagine, Cousin Elizabeth. When the fathers were arguing about breach of our betrothal contract, Joseph just stood there and said very calmly that he had this dream, and he'd decided it wasn't right to send me away, even if it could be done quietly. He said that God had sent me this child and it's going to be a son, and somehow, he's going to reconcile us all.

Please send me your blessings, and a kind word for Joseph if you have time. I trust all is well with you both. and that I can see you soon.

Mary

Letter (3)

Dearest Elizabeth,

It was so wonderful, being with you and Zacharias. Thank you for having me to stay, especially as you were confined! I was so excited to hear you have been blessed, although it must be odd not getting a word out of your husband for months on end. But a miracle, after all these years of praying and hoping.

Our children will be quite close in age, which is a nice thing for cousins. Although you and I have always dealt kindly together, and I think of you as a sister rather than a kinswoman. None of my young girl cousins were ever as kind to me.

The donkey you loaned me to bring home was very sturdy and useful, and it might be taking me on another journey soon. Joseph says we have to go to Bethlehem for the census. I tried to ask, "How can I go when I'll be so great with child? And where will we stay? The place will be *full* of descendants of King David." But he just says, "God will provide."

That's all very well, but you'd think at his age, he'd know God needs a hand sometimes. And does he plan to bring his older sons along? They must be descendants of King David, too. I guess eventually we'll have them live with us, but I want to have our baby, and get used to mothering one child, first. Joseph says that sounds reasonable, and Nathan says he's as soft as a fig about me and it won't do me any good to get my way all the time. As if that would happen.

By the time you get this, I'm hoping Joseph will have taken me to be his wife already. I'm not sorry there won't be a big wedding, but mother is being unbearable. And the women in the village, well, you'll understand how awkward it is. Whenever their gossip gets too much, I think to myself, "God has put down the mighty from their seat, and has exalted the humble and meek. He has scattered the proud in the imagination of their hearts"! That's me, humble and meek. And getting HUGE, still with months to go.

But the imagination of some of those aunties, the things they're saying about me, and about Joseph, and about some of the men in his household, and even about Roman soldiers... well, I'm glad you can't hear them. Sometimes I just look at them, and whisper, "You wait. My son is going to special. You might have your doubts, but future generations will call me blessed!" And seriously, I do feel blessed. As well as all the other feelings we talked about. About being married and a wife's duties—and a husband's—and getting to know Joseph and being mothers.

Nathan says we're a pair of impractical dreamers, and he hates to think what sort of a child we'll have or what will become of it. Sometimes I wish my brother was right, and dream of the saviour of our people appearing in our time, to change everything.

But enough daydreaming. There's much to prepare for.

Is Zacharias talking yet? How's he getting on with his Temple duties? I guess everyone knows what to do without being told. Is he being kind to you, or is he still shocked and awe-struck?

Mazel tov, dear Elizabeth. Send a message the moment you can when your child is born! I hope we won't be on the way to Bethlehem, on that not-too-uncomfortable donkey, by the time we hear from you.

Shalom, Mary

Blessings

Celestial brightness

Go in peace
into this Advent season.
Follow a star that's twinkling with courage,
blazing with possibility
to the space, the essence that is God.
And may the celestial brightness—source, spirit, sun—
be with you
enlighten, heal and empower you and those you love
this day and always.

Christmas Blessing

May the angels' message of peace and goodwill stay with us—
hearts opening
as pōhutukawa bursts into flower,
the spicy scent of pine trees fills our homes,
and angels leap off Christmas cards into our everyday lives,
affirming that we are loved and blessed.
Amen

Courage of a teenage Mary

Go in peace
and may the courage of a teenage Mary,
the loyalty of Joseph,
the grandmotherly delight of Anne,
and the fierce joy of Elizabeth
comfort and empower you;
the conception of angels,
the passion of spirit,
and the Love we call God
be with you, fulfil and liberate you
this day and always.

Hope, joy, love of Christmas

Now, go in peace
and may the Hope of Christmas inspire you
the Joy of Christmas remain with you
and the Love born at Christmas
be born again in you and those you love—
this day and always.

Amen

Blessing of Water and Spirit

(Epiphany and Baptism of Jesus)

As we end our time together
may every cloud burst be an open-air endorsement,
a baptism with dove-wings skimming the river,
whirling up a mystery, calling us Beloved.

Go in peace
replenished in water and spirit
for you have seen the star
you have heard the angels
you have gifts, given and received.

Know you are blessed, healed, loved
this day and always—
Amen

Glossary and References

Definition of te reo Māori words

These translations are from online *Māori Dictionary* and *Te Ara: The Encyclopaedia of New Zealand*

ao-mārama: world of life and light, Earth, physical world.

aroha: affection, sympathy, charity, compassion, love, empathy.

Kaumātua: Māori elders, who have many important roles in their families and nurturing the younger generations.

mahi: work, occupation

Manaakitanga: Hospitality, kindness, generosity, support - the process of showing respect, generosity and care for others.

Papatūānuku and **Ranginui:** Papatūānuku, the earth mother in Māori tradition, is seen as the birthplace of all things. Ranginui, the sky father, was torn away from Papatūānuku, the earth mother, and formed the vault of the heavens.

Tūrangawaewae is one of the most well-known and powerful Māori concepts. It is often translated as 'a place to stand'. Tūrangawaewae are places where we feel especially empowered and connected. They are our foundation, our place in the world, our home.

Whānau (verb) to be born, give birth; (noun) extended family, family group. Whānau is often translated simply as 'family', but its meaning is more complex. It includes physical, emotional and spiritual dimensions and is based on *whakapapa* (genealogy, genealogical table, lineage, descent). Whānau is based on a Māori and a tribal world view. It is through the whānau that values, histories and traditions from the ancestors are adapted for the contemporary world.

whānautanga: birth.

whare kōwhanga: birthing house.

References

Bultmann, Rudolf *New Testament and Mythology*
https://en.wikiquote.org/wiki/Rudolf_Bultmann

Great Disappointment of October 1844 and Seventh Day Adventism
wikipedia.org/wiki/Adventism

NZ Hymnbook Trust, *Carol Our Christmas*
https://pgpl.co.nz/new-zealand-hymnbook-trust-music-books-
and-cds/carol-our-christmas-details/

Parker, Dorothy "Prayer for a New Mother" in *Not so Deep as a Well*,
published by Hamish Hamilton

Pratchett, Terry *Only You Can Save Mankind*
www.terrypratchettbooks.com

Richardson, Jan *Night Visions*
www.janrichardson.com

Uris, Leon *Exodus* (1958) Doubleday & Company

Wright Edelman, Marian
www.biography.com/people/marian-wright-edelman

Thanks again

Thank you again to these faith communities

GalaXies (gay, lesbian, bisexual, transgender Christians and their families and friends) spiritual community
Ephesus Group, Wellington
and especially
St Andrew's on The Terrace Presbyterian Church

for whom most of these prayers, reflections and blessings were written and presented.

Thank you always
to my daughter Lauren Angela White,
for inspiration and shining brilliantly in my life
and
to my husband, Warwick Metcalfe—for love.

Thanks, too
to all who bought my first book, **you who delight me**, and for your encouragement to keep writing and sharing worship resources;

and to ordained and lay worship leaders who're using these liturgies to nurture inclusive, progressive faith communities.

Praise for "you who delight me"

"In this rapidly changing world where the century-old liturgies have become tired and lifeless, Bronwyn has used her poetical skill for the creation of new expressions of thanksgiving and spiritual nurture that are inspiringly fresh.

I greatly enjoyed her poem *Some ex-lovers*, and what particularly attracted me was, it's very like some of the parables of Jesus: you get to the last line—what a surprise you get!"

—*Rev Sir* **Lloyd Geering**

"Bronwyn has the creativity, imagination and power to have us sense the sacred in the ordinary. I remember when I first heard *Suddenly there is light all around* in a Christmas Eve meditation. The newborn Jesus, described in the same language that Bronwyn used for the moment of falling in love with her own child—the power of the experience of birthing brought into liturgy: earth, blood and new milk... "Bronwyn's words are more powerful and real than a thousand theological treatises on incarnation."

—*Rev Dr* **Margaret Mayman**

"Bronwyn White's first volume of poetry comes with some pretty high-powered endorsements. One of the poems has featured on National Radio, and one of New Zealand's most respected theological thinkers, Sir Lloyd Geering, offers a glowing testimonial... The second half of the book is designed for liturgical use and includes a... variety of spiritual and other subject matter."

—*Piers Fuller*, *Wairarapa News*

"What beautiful poetry! I look forward to using some of your liturgical material too."

—*Rev* **Jenny Dawson**

www.ingramcontent.com/pod-product-compliance
Lightning Source LLC
Chambersburg PA
CBHW051552120626
46551CB00013B/1489